A MOMENT'S LIFE

VOLUME 1

AAYUSH AGRAWAL

To,

The lost soul,

I consign unto thee,

This ballad of life,

A guide for your journey....

Contents

Contents

Acknowledgements

I would like to thank all my loved ones,

the people close to my heart,

my stars and the people reading this book....

Prologue

In this moment as we live and breathe,

   This defines our simple existence and our will to sustain,

   A will so strong that it drives us to an extent,

   Where the impossible seems necessary....

   They say a moment can change everything,

   some define our sanity,

   Some our faith,

   Some define our will to go on as far as it takes,

   Some, our simple acts of random kindness,

   And some, courageous acts of virtuous forgiveness....

   It is these moments which adds up to make a life-time

   And as a whole define us as a human being....

1. "OPEN-BOOK"

My life's an open book,
Hold me down and take a look....
The chapters, some are dark and bleak,
Some, a learning that you'll want to keep....
And others will simply put a smile on your face,
There's a lot of things for you to take....
lost in translation you might be,
Reading between the lines will make you see....
The pages of my life is yet to be filled,
By the journey which lies ahead of me....

2. "A PEACEFUL LIGHT"

I was a survivor in the dark world,
Which was ruled by agnostic lies;
Where there was no light,
And the only sound lingered was of agonizing cries;
Of lost souls who seek salvation from their exile....
I had a hope which kept me alive,
A hope that when I wake up tomorrow
There would be light....
And one day I thought,
Someone heard my plea,
A light shown upon me,
A peaceful light;
And I succumbed to it,
Like a little child....
'Twas so bright,
That I was blind-folded by its might;
Serenity was all in my mind....
I didn't know how joyous was I,
That I almost forgot my dark world,
And all its lies....
Happiness was bestowed upon me,
Like showers of blessings from the heavenly sky....
I realized how lonely this world could be,
And began to cry....

Suddenly a voice came from nowhere;
And spoke to me like it had known me more than I....
I backed out from my delightful thoughts,
And wondered who could it be?
It told me to believe in the divine light,
The one which now shown upon me....
It told me that it would be my guiding star,
In all of my darkest hours;
And it told me to re-establish it,
In that God-forsaken place,
From where it lost its blaze....
I did as commanded,
Man on the mission was I....
The darkness tried to sly me,
But lost its every fight;
For I now possessed the power of life....
As I re-establish the light,
All was blissful and bright;
The earth again got back its life....

3. "FINAL DESTINATION"

I was walking down the road,
So as the sun came along....
While wondering-
"What can possibly go wrong
From dusk till dawn?"
The day was finally dying,
Giving way to night,
It was the time of twilight....
The road beneath my feet,
Suddenly started to flee,
Still was all but me....
Gathering my senses back to life,
What it appeared to be a lighting strike.
I was a bit shaken but wasn't to quit,
For it was a journey I had to complete....
The night finally broke out,
And shadows of darkness started to creep....
My only hope were the stars,
Twinkling in the sky so deep.
I started following the brightest one,
For it showed me the direction,
Of my destination to reach.
Each of my senses slowly started dying,
As I'd reached a little more than my human extent.

It was as if, I was being crushed by an unknown force,
Beseeching me to repent....
But I had to go on,
Struggling till the end....
I reached my home finally,
Thanking the stars so many.
It was a victory for me,
A victory much greater than any....
My journey ended at last,
And I'll always remember it
As a token of my past....

4. "A MARINER'S DILEMMA"

These winds as they rattle the leaves,
Strike a symphony in my deserted sea of memories....
There's an ocean of thoughts inside me,
And I can sail on those waters for an eternity....
These stars as they shine in the skies so deep,
Creates a longing I am yearning to keep....
There's an ocean of thoughts inside me,
And I can sail on those waters for an eternity....
These hours as they pass by, indiscreet,
Reminds me of the moments we shared, at peace....
There's an ocean of thoughts inside me,
And I can sail on those waters for an eternity....
This night, as it transcends, torpid,
Leaves me thinking where will the future lead....
There's an ocean of thoughts inside me,
And I can sail on those waters for an eternity....

5. "DESOLATION"

My slate has been wiped cleaned,

A new life awaits to begin,

My giant palace of past,

On whose entrance once,

Stood a fountain of blissful flashbacks, vast.

Whose garden once,

Bore the fruits of happiness, cut off.

On whose walls once,

Hung the memories of a lifetime, lost.

Whose ceiling once,

Held the chandelier illuminating with hope, smashed.

Whose dark corners once,

Sheltered the demons of regret, aghast

Whose staircase once,

Led to euphoric dreams, upshot,

Whose empty rooms once,

Possessed the essence of life, surpassed,

And whose facade which,

A shadow of experience cast,l

Tumbled down and now it burns,

And from its ashes I will build a new one....

6. "PARADOX"

Too preoccupied with the current happenings,
Perhaps I've lost my roots,
Am I loosing my edge too?
Or am I finding a new one?
That remains to be seen....
Was responding to a higher calling,
Before the occurrence of fate,
And as much as I'd like to believe in it,
My perceptions have changed;
I now want to believe in choices,
For they ultimately lead you there
And for all of that, I need to go back,
To visit the ghosts of my past,
And going back, a familiar sense of nostalgia takes over,
It is as if I'm seeing my past through a kaleidoscope,
Those vibrant, rustic, moving images filled with hope,
They keep pulling me lower and lower down below....
A silhouette from the depths emerges,
"Follow me..." - it urges,
It takes me through a series of memories,
Untill I find the one which I need and together we,
Ascend towards the consciousness gradually....

7. "A TRAGIC COMEDY"

'Was standing over the edge,
Thoughts running deep,
Have had nothing my whole life,
But promises to keep,
Realizing now with my eyes shut,
I've been chewed like the cud....
Helped all I could, crossing every line,
Everything was lost what was once mine,
Filled with hope, head held up high,
Didn't know, was living a monstrous lie,
Jumped into the waging war,
Trapped in the sands of time,
A mountain of emotions waiting to erupt,
As I've been chewed like the cud....

8. "LIMBO"

I'm a lonely soul wandering the vastness deep,
Nor the path, neither my future is foreseen....
These seconds as they pass by,
Add up to the moments of a lifetime....
A man bearing his heart out fancied a crime,
For this deed must I, be shackled into solitude,
And roam the depths of this purgatory....
The conscious in denial, remains to muse,
And with the coming days, comes more misery....
The days are darker same as night,
But this inner voice insists to put a fight....
So I stand, with a sword in hand,
Set to slay the demons inside,
And slay did I till none remained,
Now I'm free....

9. "BLUE FUNK"

My life is hanging by a thin line
Lost are the things dear to me
What were once mine...
Bleak is the boulevard, nothing I could see...
Times are darkest as the clouds above,
Thundering, roaring, so are my thoughts...
The world once I knew was beautiful, full of love,
Now it seems to be morbid, dull and lost...
We wish things to be alright when all hope's gone...
Out of all the things we choose to do,
There's a fine line between right and wrong
The consequences of our actions defines the truth...
Hope seems to be distant,
Distant are the stars shining bright...
All I have to be is persistent,
And I'll see another morning's light....

10. "QUALM"

Abandon all hope and wish to die,
The last attempt to escape a lie,
Living like there's no tomorrow,
Life's miseries and all its sorrows...
Guilt, regret- the heart-brake's aftermath
Takes you high and drops you flat
An undying urge to go back and start all over again
Was present at the center of it, when it all began...
A simple gift of happiness to you,
Acts of random kindness you do...
Memories haunting you in the middle of the night
Lying wide awake consumed by fright...
Relieved to see the morning light,
Dawns a new day brisk and bright....

11. "UTOPIA"

I yearn for a world beyond the reach of mortal eyes,
Bathed in stardust,
Surrounded by the nebula of a rising star's light,
Where the droplets of eternal waterfall shine
Like crystals, they lit up the heavenly skies....
A place where titans and men accompany the divine;
Whence hailed the angels and now it's a shrine....
I speak incoherently perhaps,
Or it can be a distant, Utopian future nevertheless....
My words maybe rumbled, but my thoughts are just fine;
To paint this picture in my mind's eye,
I went into the deepest roots of my thoughts where they all lie,
'Twas then, I was bestowed with this vision,
Breaking me free from my delusion,
The path is clear now, walking between the fine line,
I ascend to the crown - abode of the divine....

12. "MAN OF VIRTUE"

A man so lost in his thoughts,
Reels back to his senses;
As the world around him,
Rejects him and his false offences.
"Time has changed you…"- They say,
"We don't need you anymore…"- They say….
It is very accurate that when a valuable
Kept too long in possession,
Looses its significance….
It was about time that he learned a lesson.
He had given so much for his people,
And never asked anything in return…
For all that he was adorned…
But his glory days were over,
And about that he was well confirmed…
With that he took a leap of faith,
And dived into the ocean….
Thinking he would return
Maybe in another life,
Maybe in another time,
So his eminence would be attained….

13. "DEMENTIA"

His conscious, now slipping into a greater sense of dementia,
His thoughts, transcending into an archaic void
Which reveals itself on a diurnal basis;
His eyes, gradually loosing somnolence
Wondering about the commotion in an unconscious mind
An inevitable comrade of the forthcoming adversary....
It's funny how life at its peak of euphoria,
Tumbles down into the valley of grief....
And he amidst all experiencing an adrenaline rushed joyride....
Thought 'twas just a drifting cloud,
As there are always sunny days after a stormy night
But his sun was yet to shine,
The night was both, morbid and malign...
He didn't let his ship sink,
For his heart was full of hope and his eyes- unflinching
Kept his vessel steady, pushing away all the insanity
He reached the shore ultimately,
And led a life of harmony....

14. "INVINCIBLE"

Fear has no meaning unless it conquers you,
This demon inside him, had captured him though,
And day by day it grows,
Reaming its roots into his soul...
His vain - its branches, in them runs gall...
He had lived through an eternity and there's an eternity ahead,
Which is not enough, for he has too large a debt...
Betrayed by the world, he besought asylum,
The darkness embraced him, misdeed had been done...
Now it follows him - his deviltry shadow,
No matter how far he runs...
It cursed him with endless anguish yet blessed him with infinite
power,
But it forgot, his heart was pure and far too courageous to cower....
He looked at the sun one last time and leaped into the unknown,
With a sword of zeal and the armor of hope, bright as they shone...
Banished by light, he suddenly started to dissipate,
And so the demon within as he was ruling his own fate...
The sword and armor - his remains,
And he - a symbol, invincible in these terrains....

15. "A VIRTUOSO'S PEREGRINATION"

He stood there caressing the crevasses of the canvas,
With every inch of his fingers, he craft,
He let it all out - his emotions, his sentiments...
And in those moments he reincarnated renaissance
There stood a masterpiece so magnificent
As if created by the Almighty Himself....
The world was about to go head over heels just to see,
His time had come, there awaited his glory...
He finally found the purpose of his life
What he was born to do and strived
All those soul-searching, seeking redemption,
Had yielded a fruit, a fruit of salvation....
The only thing stood between him and his destiny was his alter-ego,
As his battle with himself had began years ago....
Every time he created something, the other him destroyed it,
And every time he tried to conquer it, he lost his every fight....
And again the other him lit the canvas on fire and it was consumed
by light,
But this opus of his was so pure, as if he had created life...
It rose from the ashes like Phoenix and shone bright,
His alter-ego couldn't believe this anomaly and met his demise....

16. "JACK FROST"

His body stood still,
Like a numb tree in a windswept winter,
Covered with snow all over....
A gush of wind,
As if an invisible enemy
Came rushing in,
Shuddering doors and windows as many
And old bones rattled like parchment drums....
The evening was just young
Dwelling a full course of night ahead...
His only ally was the flickering light,
Endowing him with a snatch of warmish complacency.
Reviving his faith to persist...
Strong was his will, more than his nemesis...
He swore to strive, no matter how much the frost prolonged
Only one thought occupied his mind -
He would live to see the dawn....

17. "ATTAINMENT"

The things we did in our wake,
Are nothing but memories made...
One day our actions would justify our existence,
As on that day we would face our annihilation....
And in awe of everything,
There would be another inception....
A new life with a new fervor would perish,
And along with them the world would cherish....
The things they do in their wake,
Would be nothing but memories made...
A whole new era of transformation would prevail,
Change would sow the seeds of ingenuity and foretell
Our morrow, so we would brace our prudence
And do things in our wake
Which would be nothing but memories made.....

18. "THE PROCEEDINGS OF NIGHT"

The night's being too long,
Insomnolence is starting to take over its toll…
Sleepless in my bed, 'er the sheets as I roll;
My eyes, like dead empty sockets…bleak,
In them, not a bit of sleep…
Until the breaking up of dawn,
The darkness slowly fades,
Recollecting all of its shades,
And those shadows lurking behind the curtains,
Hunting me, I couldn't be more certain…
The acute silence at the dead of the night,
Could be blessing for one,
And for one, it could be fright…
I find solace in it,
For it is my only expedient,
Of isolating from this world,
And from all of its fictive fabrication,
That binds these people,
And masks them from the Omniscient.…

19. "FAIRY-TALE"

A solitary soul wandering the horizons,
His life - an upheaval of emotional confusion....
Met a damsel who's story was fairly alike...
Became the center of his life's circle,
With everything revolving around in an endless coil...
Couldn't care less, as time tends to slow down at the center,
They had it all, they had each other....
But the orbit now and then kept changing over and over....
Raised by anguish and agony, his thoughts ran in that direction,
She kept the spark of life alive in him,
In return, he tried giving her all the attention....
A clockwork of mutual astuteness
Is what kept their endearment poised
The sound of all the commotion was now music to their ears,
Life suddenly seemed so simple,
They won every battle without even putting up a fight.....
Some say happiness is being content,
But that's the blessing they were yet to receive....
However, they found their mountain top eventually;
And together they lived ever after happily.....

20. "MARVEL"

The day began, the Apollonian,
Did his usual heliolatry.....
That serene energy, that pure, limitless light,
Could bestow him with strength extraordinary....
He was a pagan, the sun his deity,
Eternal was his devotion, an undying fidelity....
Same the goddess meant to the moon rather beyond it,
The moon's love for the goddess was amaranthine....
Time runs its course, night started dwelling;
The moon shone bright, his very existence was her light....
He was an ugly dark orb, wandering in the vastness, deep,
Until she turned him into a majestic celestial being,
Now her light was his to keep....
The moon announced his liege allegiance to the goddess,
And it was for an eternity to be....
But the Apollonian abhorred the night and the moon's light,
For it was stolen or so he thought,
As he was a loon to fathom their endearment....
The aggravating uneasiness started devouring him,
So he roved the north to find the midday sun,
And upon finding it, he conceived that the goddess was his,
But the universe had other plans....
As a pristine sentiment could transcend any immeasurable amount
of distance,

Moon, her paramour had come to claim his meed,
And the world would bask in their eclipse....
A divine convergent of the gods;
There he stood awe-stricken,
Witnessing the charismatic phenomenon,
That austere coup of unparalleled ardor,
Defying his very axiom about the sun....
As far as the zeal of a man could take him, his reached the end,
He was enlightened now; they were the gods of the cosmos,
And being a mere man, he made peace with his vanity,
And worshiped them both coequally....

21. "SUNSHINE"

To love you is to kiss that morning dew
Like a fresh breath of sunshine...
Which mesmerizes me every time...
And makes me feel in the presence of the divine....
To love you is to watch that dream come true,
Which I've longed for an eternity...
Catch my breath, as I do,
There's a whole new reality...
To love you is to feel that never-ending warmth,
Which revives my heart every time it slows down
Giving me reason to live before this moment's gone...
And here I am, praying that this night shouldn't see the dawn...
To love you is to feel that blessing which was about time I
received....
And the bond we share....I found a new world which we are in....
You are my beginning, you are my end and there's no place I'd
rather be....

22. "YEARNING"

There was a time when my day used to start with the sound of your
voice,
There was a time when your smiles used to set everything alright,
In my bleakest moments, in my darkest night,
You came as this 'celestial angel' and saved my life;
You made me shine with your light....
Some say when you truly, deeply, love a person,
It's more then just an affection and in doing so,
You touched my soul and it was divine....
But that didn't last very long,
The distance parted us and our priorities took height....
The days are darker now, I'm looking for your light,
Each moment seems a million years,
And your memories still lingers in my mind,
It can't be undone, I am fighting to survive,
Just some hope that there will come those times again,
So that I can relive them and create even better memories to hold
on to....is all I want from this life,
And just some hope that there is a better tomorrow
Is all I have to win this fight....

23. "SOMNOLENCE"

Sleep, sleep into a good night,
These wounds would heal with time,
And all your worries would disappear,
By the morning's first light....
Sleep, sleep into a good night....
This night would take you through,
To a land where all your dreams would come true,
Where all your distress would fade,
Into a cloud drifting up in its flight....
Sleep, sleep into a good night...
With all your strength fight,
These demons with all your might,
Don't let the flame of hope,
Burn out in theses darkest time....
Sleep, sleep into a good night....
You'll emerge victorious,
Courageous and glorious,
And once again you'll cherish your life....
Sleep, sleep into a good night....

24. "IN TIME"

In time we smile, cherishing the blissful memories,
Of the childhood, we still have a longing for...
In time we weep, regretting the dreadful deeds,
Of the past hoping, never to face it anymore...
In time we love, enjoying the warm company,
Of our dear ones, praying to never let them go...
In time we sulk, cursing the selfish world in agony,
Of its self-esteemed people, getting themselves so low...
In time we dare, speaking up our brave heart,
Of its wish, expecting it to be heard over all...
And in time we prevail, living inanimately to depart,
From this world, waiting for our fall....

25. "INCEPTION"

Once again, as I pick up this pen,
My thoughts start running deep
How can HE - the ALMIGHTY,
Bless us with such powers - it amazes me,
The miraculous phenomenon of creating life
Was given to each living thing and unbiased was HE....
Born are the flowers rejoicing in the sunlight
Born are magnificent creatures in deep blue sea
Born are the wild ones in dense canopy,
Dwelling their life in congeniality....
And fancying a life in harmony born were we....
I cherish each moment of this life,
For this has been a blessing throughout for me,
And I hope you cherish yours wishing you-
A happy beginning....